Volume 75 of the Yale Series of Younger Poets

WILLIAM VIRGIL DAVIS

One Way to Reconstruct the Scene

FOREWORD BY RICHARD HUGO

New Haven and London, Yale University Press, 1980

Published with assistance from
the Mary Cady Tew Memorial Fund

Designed by Sally Harris
and set in Monotype Bembo type
by Heritage Printers, Inc., Charlotte, N.C.
Printed in the United States of America by
The Murray Printing Co., Westford, Mass.

Published in Great Britain, Europe, Africa, and
Asia (except Japan) by Yale University Press,
Ltd., London. Distributed in Australia and
New Zealand by Book & Film Services, Artarmon,
N.S.W., Australia; and in Japan by Harper & Row,
Publishers, Tokyo Office.

Library of Congress Cataloging in Publication Data

Davis, William Virgil, 1940–
    One way to reconstruct the scene.

    (Yale series of younger poets ; v. 75)
    I. Title. II. Series.
PS3554.A938305   811'.5'4   79-22810
ISBN 0-300-02502-5
ISBN 0-300-02503-3 pbk.

For My Mother and Father

Contents

III

IV

Although I hear echoes of Yeats and Roethke in the work of William Virgil Davis, and even though he writes a poem about Wallace Stevens, an elegy for John Berryman, and dedicates a poem to Elizabeth Bishop, he seems to have already moved beyond immediate influences. If I were to compare Davis with any poet it would be with Edwin Muir. Although their poems are different, the two have much in common that is important.

In their poems, both Davis and Muir exhibit an integrity of spirit, a willingness to submit their words to the configurations of what lies inside them and is eligible for a poem, eligible that is within limits of self-imposed private standards. Davis finds, as Muir found, writing difficult, and in their poems both poets refuse to ignore, escape, or minimize their difficulties. In other words, both are poets of honor. And while honor may be graying at the edges these days, for me the honor found in the poems of Muir and Davis more than compensates for the occasional poem that does less than I'd hoped, for lack of surface dazzle, for execution that now and then approaches the awkward, and for lapsing once in awhile into literary or "poetic" phrasing.

W. H. Auden pointed out somewhere that a lyric poet must accept the world exactly as he finds it, and I'd add that that can be helpful, at least for the duration of the poem. Auden might have added that the poet has an obligation not to *render* the world the way he found it. William Virgil Davis is a poet who, when he writes, contends with a loving self who wants to render the world as found. His battle is the classic one, the memory versus the imagination.

Sometimes Davis will submit himself to idealism and call idealism memory, letting the real memory believe *it* is what is controlling him ("Another Night with Snow"). Davis's sophistication is usually more philosophical than artistic, a mark of his intellectual maturity. When he says "This is more than memory" ("A Triptych for My Father") he is acknowledging the nature of his ever-present potential for artistic failure.

Despite Davis's awareness of his own creative problems he seldom writes about aesthetic matters. He acknowledges one in "The Cat in the Snow," a poem about Wallace Stevens and one of *his* aesthetic principles. In another poem, "Mexico, My Friend," Davis recognizes that a free-floating impulse to write results in words that need to attach to a subject, especially when the remembrance that ignited that impulse is itself of little importance to the writer. Words found this way have more warmth than their immediate sources and must have an audience, a place or person to play to. That accounts for the ambiguity of "My Friend," which is both Mexico and the reader.

Sometimes Davis finds himself in a world religious with accommodation and benevolent possession. In a poem that reminds me a bit of Roethke, "After the Funeral," Davis locates a scene of renewals, stable relationships, receptivity, and joy, a scene Roethke might have found replayed in childhood, and one Davis finds worthy of adult celebration

> I had learned the secret
> of the pool, the borrowed depth which kept it full.

And it is adult to realize we lose loved ones and escape emptiness by acknowledging what we took from them while they were alive.

Like most poets, Davis has his obsessions, among them bones and rooms. For him, bones serve as metaphors for a variety of human characteristics. Sometimes the bones are independent in spirit and as compelling and fascinating as heroes are to a child

("Following the Bones"). Sometimes, being that part of our body that survives longest, they become emblematic of our capacity for psychic and spiritual survival ("After Three Days"). When fear forces our retreat, the bones can represent something almost religious in us, even faith itself, that can stand for us in our need ("The Bones in Search of a Bed"). Bones can even die for us, like cheerful martyrs ("Renting My Bed to the Bones").

Rooms seem to act as metaphors for human interiors that can: diminish existential possibilities ("In a Room"); house our desire to live and make social contact ("That House, This Room"); provide a place that even if not totally familiar renders the threatening world temporarily harmless ("A Room without Windows").

But of all obsessions, memory itself remains the most persistent, the most demanding. Some tricks Davis plays to gain his release from memory may be minor and even lighthearted, but at least one is major and serious: having the imagination masquerade itself as memory. In the title poem, Davis reconstructs the scene of a disaster, an auto wreck, not by changing the details to make the aftermath more palatable the second time, but by leading up to the final scene with bits of information about the victims while still alive immediately before the crash. After the crash, the details, unaltered actually, but verbally rearranged, the grim aftermath becomes—no pun intended—a memorable still life. It is a triumph of art over death, a poem that works, like all good poems, for reasons that remain mysteriously buried in the poem and in ourselves.

But it also is the triumph of imagination over memory and for Davis that is the most difficult battle he has to fight. "Memory is the first property of loss" Davis tells us ("Property of Loss")— and that may be true. At least it is worth considering. Certainly a scene, no matter how unattractive initially, reconstructed lovingly in active language posing as passive recall is a true property of gain. Davis believes in and works to create a world we can humanely attend the second time around, and his poems often provide that second chance.

Richard Hugo

Acknowledgments

Acknowledgment is made to the following publications for poems, some in earlier versions, which originally appeared in them.

Arts in Society: "In the Pit"
The Atlantic Monthly: "One Way to Reconstruct the Scene"
The Chariton Review: "A Short History of Misunderstanding,"
  "Breakfast as a Last Resort"
The Dalhousie Review: "My Son in Snow"
Denver Quarterly: "The Time of Year, the Hour,"
  "That House, This Room"
The Georgia Review: "Short Treatise on the Hand"
The Massachusetts Review: "Driving Alone in Winter"
Moons and Lion Tailes: "A Bucket of Water"
New England Review: "Snow," "The Sleep of the Insomniac"
Perspective: "Following the Bones," "Some Things the Bones
  Never Know"
Poem: "The Bones at Rest"
Poetry: "After the Funeral," "In a Room"
Poetry Northwest: "The Bones in Search of a Bed," "Meeting
  the Bones," "Renting My Bed to the Bones"
The Sewanee Review: "A Late Elegy for John Berryman,"
  "A Triptych for My Father"
Shenandoah: "Not Many Years"
Southern Poetry Review: "The Oxygen Tent"
The Wallace Stevens Journal: "The Cat in the Snow"

I

Another Night with Snow

It is March, 1940. I am not born.
It snows all night. Snow more than a foot
deep between the houses. Trees

holding it along their arms' length.
My father walks slowly home
from the factory, his black lunch box

under his arm, his hands stuffed
deep in his pockets, his red scarf
wrapped twice around his throat.

My mother, big with me, waits
behind the window. Her breath blossoms,
flowers the glass. She has just

put the coffee on. She is anxious
because of the snow, me, my father's coat,
so thin. Last year there was little

work. Now all the extra money, I know,
will go for me. I kick, and turn
over. My mother puts her hand down

and pats me carefully. I see her smile.
She has so much to think about.
The bread wagon comes around the corner

and stops. The horses stamp the snow
and snort over their shoulders. The heat
rises from their haunches as my mother and I

watch them and wait. I think the horses
are wonderful. When my father sees us,
he waves. His scarf blows out behind him.

He is smiling, happy. My mother waves
back, watching him come closer.
He stops to buy a loaf of bread and tucks

it under his other arm. It is still warm.
My father's face is strong. I whisper
to my mother how happy I am.

My father winks at me and kisses my mother.
We stand at the window and watch
the snow fall slowly through the years.

After the Funeral

When the stone falls the water rises up
to meet it, to cup it in its hand and close
upon it like a fist. The ripples spread
outward from the spot where the stone sinks and then
return to calm, and, disappearing, hold
the water level of the pond. After the funeral
I walked the edge of water dropping stones
in the pond. Each time, beyond the blurring, my
face came back together in the mirror
of water, trees grew again, the sky held fast
in place.

         I found a pool off to the side
of the pond. Rock had reared and cut the water
off to leave the pool, isolate and small,
protected by the rock, part of the pond.

Was there some secret seepage beneath the rock
which kept it full? Some private spring? I sat
upon a stone to think things out. Later,
the wind came up. The trees along the pond
were bent to the breaking point. The water stirred
and it seemed that, all at once, the pond took life.
Waves, like hands beneath a sheet, began
to move across the lately silent surface.

Then rain came, great droplets. The pond rose up
to meet them, took them in, and lifting from its bed
began to sing. The waves washed against the rock
divide, washed over it and fell into the pool
beside me. They set the puddle moving
with their rhythm and now it rose and fell as well.

And then, all at once, the storm had passed. The sky
cleared, the waves shrank down again and leveled
off. The sun appeared. The rock ridge shined
and dried. The water in the small pool was calm.

I stood up and dropped a stone into the pool.
I waited for the ripples to disappear,
and then I started home. I had learned the secret
of the pool, the borrowed depth which kept it full.

A Triptych for My Father

I

Bent low above the old piano, his eyes closed,
my father leans into the only tune he knows.
Snow catches in the corners of the windows.

The patterned panes are more than half erased
by the intricate embroidery of ice which traces
the glass. The firelight falls full upon his face.

II

On a clear cold morning in late autumn he led
the hogs out and brought the hammer down hard,
in one quick stroke. The ground puddled with blood,

but they fell without feeling anything. The cut
breath, rising slowly from each purpled snout,
caught in the crisp air like an afterthought.

III

This is more than memory. Tonight, unable to sleep,
I sit watching snow fall slowly through the deep
trees outside the window. The fire falls in a heap.

I cannot kill him off. His face is traced in the window,
watching me. The long wind whistles in the old piano.
The room is alive with lost music, in diminuendo.

View from the Backyard

Each evening at this hour, birds weave the air.
Birds of all kinds, some so high I can hardly
make them out, faint flutterings, like shadows
moving together to close before they fall.
They make such steady noise, like real silver
spoons clattering in teacups, the old ladies
propped up around the room, their hats on
and gloves, the shades all tightly drawn.

My son, only one year, hears the birds, looks
up, points, says what he says for everything.
My wife says such ceremonies have something
to do with the season, the coming migrations,
the getting together of the flocks. It is
as good as any guess I have and so we let
it go at that, not really wanting to know,
knowing all creatures deserve their secrets.

In the darkened room the old ladies speak in
whispers and grotesque expressions take the place
of overt gestures, always impolite. Their hats
are always changing and although no one speaks
of it everyone takes note. The air is heavy
with perfume and stale flower smells. The tea
was never tea and all the old girls are dead.

The circles seem to begin closing in, at each
turn tightening. It is not possible to keep
one single bird in focus while it describes one
sweep of the circle. The sound, with the dark,
increases steadily, by the hour, by the day.
One evening, no doubt soon, when we least expect
it, the birds will suddenly be gone. My son
will stare in vain. My wife will say I told you
so, and turn away. The old ladies in the same
drawing room are dancing on the high-backed chairs.

My Son in Snow

I bring him back from death.
My son, a child of three,
inhabits my mind
this winter day,
caught up in snow.

He is here, playing
in the snow, giving
snow a shape he knows.
His breath blurs and blows
away in the wind.
His snowman stands
in our backyard.

Then the game changes.
He runs and,
twisting in midair,
he leaps and falls
out full upon his back,
winding his arms
to make an angel,
laughing, beginning
to rise. Spent,

he falls asleep
in the snow, his arms
still ready to rise.
I step up to him
and bend down to lift him
from the shape he's made,
his image frozen
in this snow, my mind.

An Overcast Day in Late Autumn

for Elizabeth Bishop

I have seen silver trays pass into oblivion
and old men cough in corridors or stumble
on walks wet with rain. Nothing changes enough.

The breakfast toast refuses to be delivered.
The tea is weak and cold. Each day, Elizabeth,
with so much ceremony, all the morning papers

report the same stale news. As I write this,
a dull rain continues. Through my window I watch
gulls rise, blend in with the sky above the bay.

Winter Light

All night through the dark the dark
is falling. Dead limbs fill with water,
freeze in the hard light of winter.

Out walking this early morning, I stop,
stoop, stare at my own reflection,
bent like a branch is bent by water.

Driving Alone in Winter

Driving alone in winter through acres of land
deserted by everything save the snow
trapped in the ruts of the road,
the moon broken by the bare trees,
I remember the days when my brothers and I would fall asleep
in the backseat on the way home.

Tonight, coming home, I remember
the faint light on the dashboard holding my father's face,
my mother's soft voice, my brothers asleep,
the moon running among the trees beside the car.

The Sleep of the Insomniac

The body beside your body sleeps like death.

There is nothing to hear from your heart,
ghostly clock, full of collapse. Even your
breath, wind from the world's wind, breaks

unevenly, losing itself in itself. Suddenly,

the stars fall to fill your room. Time is
the thin spider you found along the fence
when you were five and kept to yourself

the way, for years, you kept your body

inviolate until you learned there was nothing
to be done for the flesh which would keep it
incorruptible. Death is as close as the wife

you sleep beside. Stars fasten to your forehead.

The Oxygen Tent

Always in the dark rooms the sheets
seemed alive. Forced to keep awake,
to keep conscious, forced to watch
the constant rise and fall of the lung
which hung around me like a shroud
(that strange amorphous body breathing
with me) there were times in the middle
of cold winter nights when I believed
I had stopped breathing. Then the sheets
would rise up suddenly and begin
to dance in the dark. Watching them,
I would imagine myself under water,
caught in an airtight, transparent casket,
watching the floodlights splinter
on the dark surface of the water,
draining down to dark above me
where I waited, out of sight, moving
with the water while they kept dragging
the river, dragging all night, missing me.

Property of Loss

If you can't find the book or your face
in the mirrored morning above your razor,
take a turn in the garden. There
the mock orange, grown out of all control,
stands brazen in her own perfume, attracting
winged insects. She takes no notice
how a butterfly with a beautiful eyespot
is killed by the cat not four feet away.

You must try to remember what it all
reminds you of . . . How many years
has it been since you took up the pipe?
Not even the teeth remember. Memory
is the first property of loss.
When you reach and take your handkerchief
from your pocket, will you notice
how the image imprinted on it,
like your shadow on the sidewalk before you
when you step from a darkened doorway
into the sunlight, fits perfectly
against the confines of your face?

II

The Cat in the Snow

One morning, before morning, Wallace Stevens,
asleep in Hartford, awoke, several hours before
daylight, and listened to a cat crossing crisp
snow beneath his window. The cat moved almost
inaudibly, he tells us. The fact that Stevens
chose to write about this cat crossing the snow
in an essay on the irrational element in poetry
is irrational, just as poetry itself is irrational.
There is no subject beyond the cat running on the snow
in the moonlight beneath his window, Stevens said.

A Late Elegy for John Berryman

Admit
that poetry is one of the dangerous trades.
No matter how many we know who have been goaded
by its black promises to deliver
their bodies to the blue snowdrift of death,
it was not poetry, but life, they died of.
            —Peter Davison

Ice floes form on the Chicago River,
passing under the bridges along Wacker Drive.
An old man, hunched inside his overcoat,
the collar turned up, his cap pulled down,
stumbles against the storm, breathing
under his breath some scraps of song.

He struggles against the wind and steadies
himself on a pole, pausing in the spot of light
just long enough to lower his tone and take up
another voice, as if in conversation
with himself. Ahead of him, the red lights
on top of the tallest building in the world
wink at him and he winks back at them
and continues, more slowly, along the snow-
covered street, as precariously balanced
as a clown walking an imaginary line
through the center of the center ring.
An expert in unease, practiced in his art
and awkward act, he comes toward me
through the snow, covered with snow.
Thinking he might be dangerous, I turn
and cross to the other side of the street.

John, I never knew you, but knew you
were born against yourself. Even your name
against you from the start . . .

I had a student once, old enough to be
my mother, who said, after a reading,
you cried yourself to sleep in her lap.
She knew enough of poetry to know
you were not mad, but she wouldn't sleep
with you. I wish she had.

                        The third
anniversary of your death approaches,
like an old man walking above icy water,
staggering against the wind here in
a windy city four hundred miles south
of Minneapolis. The metaphor he makes,
mixed with your memory, has stunned me
into speech.

                        The old man continues
slowly up the street, moving through
circles of light. As we are about to pass,
each on our own side of the street,
he stops and lifts his head and stares,
then waves, then goes on on his way.
Thinking of you, even after he has turned
his back, I turn and wave him on.

January

One morning I awoke and found that it had been snowing all night inside my body. The snow was still falling, filtering down through my ribs, filling in my arms and legs. Already my feet were full. In the left leg the snow was as deep as the knee, as if I had stepped into a hole.

Then I could no longer move. My legs were too heavy, weighted with the snow. When I tried to speak I found my tongue swollen, my mouth frozen shut. It was only January and I had promised to visit a young woman who lived alone in one room above a garage. She had long black hair and never laughed. She must be wondering what happened to me.

Spider

The web outside the window filled
with first light, the dew like small rain
stopped to seize the morning. We lie awake
without speaking or smoking. We have been together
this whole night, and never another.
That we both know.
Soon, the spider crouches, still, waiting,
off center but central in the web.
All the lines around him run through
his own wet eyes
and he waits for what the wind will deliver.

The Ring Tree

I see her face in silhouette, against the glass
where light has lightly touched
and wind turned back my mind to this room
I almost remember. On the bureau,
in white, as the room is white, a small china
tree stands, solitary, bare.

There is nothing there. The delicate twiglike limbs
of the tree stretch forth,
as if in winter, toward snow. While
I watch, remembering, the ring tree shifts
in the dimmed light and I see
a young woman's hand stretched toward me.

A Bucket of Water

A young woman sits by the well
in the center of the square.
She has just drawn a bucket of water
and watched an insect cross
the length of a small piece of wood.

If she were at home she would
lie naked in her bed and wait
for her man to return from the fields.
She would sing to him.
They would both be naked.

She lifts the bucket of water
and begins to sing to herself
as she starts toward her house.
She sings a sad song without words
and transfers the bucket
from one hand to the other.

Mexico, My Friend

I am thinking this afternoon
of a woman dying in Mexico.

She will not remember me
although we met once, lived

in the same small town for several
years, had the same friends.

I played poker with her husband,
who usually lost, as he lost her,

although she keeps his name.
I understand that she has married

again. I did not love her
and do not begrudge this fact.

I have never been to Mexico,
although I once hoped to be

a matador. Even this cold
wet afternoon is irrelevant,

I must admit, just a poor
excuse for a chain of words

which have to have some start,
some place to begin to get where

they want to get. In this case
that is Mexico, my friend.

Come Home

The butt against your shoulder
rests easy, the clean, oiled wood

against your cheek as soft
as a glove, your elbow at rest

on your knee, your left hand
cupped beneath the barrel,

your breath as easy as sleep
or death, as natural as love,

as inevitable as revenge,
you wait behind the door

in the dark room, listen
like an animal for the first

evidence of familiar feet
come home, come home at last.

One Way to Reconstruct the Scene

The moon, through light snow, between the trees,
distorted by the broken glass, looked blue,
almost the color of the girl's blue dress,
or the man's eyes. The car came to rest
against the large maple forty yards from the road,
bisecting the angle of the slow curve beyond the bridge.

The girl was thrown free. She lay as if asleep
against the tree, her hands in her lap.
Perhaps she was dreaming. The man was still
behind the wheel, his hand to his head, a cup
of blood spilled over his yellow shirt. The brake
pedal was pushed all the way through the floorboard.

It was winter. A light snow fell past her window.
She had been waiting for hours. When he came
she had fallen asleep. She dreamed she was dreaming.
He whispered and she awakened. She smiled.
They sat watching snow fall through the trees,
the moon move slowly across the sky. They spoke.

He knew the road by heart. His father had helped
to build the bridge. They were speaking softly together.
The faint blue light reflected from the snow
as it fell slowly through the trees made the blue
of her dress bluer. They did not speak of the night,
no doubt they hardly noticed. There was nothing to know

It happened without warning. There, suddenly,
outlined in the dark like an animal only visible
when it turns to let you see its eyes, a shape
of something insubstantial cut off his view
as he started to turn, beyond the bridge, just
into the long slow curve. He tried to blink it back.

The girl in the blue dress leaned against the tree.
She seemed to be sleeping. The man remained in the car,
upright, his blue eyes open. Light snow fell slowly
through the barren limbs of the tree above the car.
The moon moved across the sky. It cast a light blue
reflection on the scene, the snow, the broken glass.

The Weight Lifter

Only the weight awaits him. There is nothing
to know. He has only one thing to do. Now,
already, he stands over it, breathing deeply,
then bending, waiting, until, in one instant
of motion, in a blur too quick to be seen, he
lifts it above his head, holds it.

                                          One summer
he ran with his father through flower-filled
fields, the wind among them, turning them,
his heart in his head, his breath like lead,
his legs lost to only the running, the wind,
the fields filled with flowers, his father.

Blood squirts from one of his eyes but he
does not blink. Instead, he stands motionless,
not thinking of anything, not even the weight.
He feels something small spin around
in his head. He steps from under the weight
and throws it, like a thing, to the floor.

If they ever existed, the fields and flowers
faded long ago. For the old man, alone with
his memories, time is like the broken clock
beside the faded photograph on the mantle.
In the mist of a misty morning he walks
quietly along a lonely road in a white winter.

The Leaving

The light lasted on the window,
on the sill. The room was already empty,
abandoned by everything save one gray glove
fallen, fisted and forgotten,
by the side of an empty jardiniere.
The wind blew in from the water
like a landowner. The wagon had been hitched
for hours. The horses stood in the snow
stamping, twitching their ears in the wind.

An Odor of Chrysanthemums

Invariably, the room was earthy. There was little
for us to say. We repeated the names, testing our
breath against the odor of chrysanthemums. We spoke
of irrelevant things, not worth repeating. The room
was small, stuffy. The chrysanthemums were yellow
and red. The day was gray, overcast. By afternoon,
a steady drizzle began, as predicted. People we
didn't remember came and went quietly. We spoke
softly and nodded, smiling. Men in dark suits stood
along the walls and blinked when the clock chimed.
Everyone knew exactly what to do. The walls were off-
white. No one spoke of chrysanthemums as inappropriate.

III

Following the Bones

The bones do not remember the soft skin
surrounding them

they pull the dark blood from the skin
and stand up on their own

they walk in the shapes of shadows
and shine in the dark wind

I've followed them
even though I do not know where they're going

Meeting the Bones

The bones are drunk again
as night falls as shadows
step into shadows and the bells
in the old church tower
announce midnight I hear
them coming before I see them
they stop to rest every few feet
fall against lampposts trip
over curbs moving slowly
into view they lurch
down the dimly-lighted street
in search of sleep

Just as we are about to collide
I step aside to let them pass

The next thing I know
I awaken behind a row of bushes
not far from a small circle
of light at the edge
of the park a policeman
stands over me his flashlight
bent to my face the faint
fall of a fountain overflowing
in the distance he bends
down to test my breath and asks
me my name and where I live
he asks me what happened
I fix my face in a smile
and tell him I don't remember
the bones inside me are laughing

They Gather Together

Those that were broken by life
are made whole
those who lost limbs
have their limbs restored
those born deformed
remain deformed
but no one speaks of it

They gather together in the early light of morning
they begin marching
move in tune with a silent song

They gather momentum
their ranks swell with the music

They maneuver to let others in
amending their ranks
as they go
singing
their ranks swelling with the music

Any distortions are deliberate

After Three Days

After three days without water or shelter
alone on the empty sand
with only the stale wind for companion

when anyone else would have given up

the bones grit their teeth
spit at death
and drink away the dark

In the Pit

In the pit
in the deep dark of the earth
where there is no light
where even the wind whispers
and only the oldest stones
dare to speak
blind worms
move slowly over the bones
and create
with their intricate embroidery
a moving tapestry
the model of a mind
articulately arranged

The Promise

And if one day we will rise
do not let the light know
or the ground which covers us
which was always warm
or even this song we sing
this sad long song no
do not let it know

Let it come if it comes
like unexpected water when roots
are dry like lightning
in a calm summer sky
or animals new-born stepping out
on new-fallen snow or
breath where no lungs are

The Bones in Search of a Bed

A hand comes up the banister
outside the bedroom door
they hesitate
the wind hushes
under the door
and the angle of light
opens slowly

I slide over the side
of the bed
and pull myself in
under it the bones
stop beside the side
of the bed and the bed
takes their weight
like a shadow disappearing
in the dark

they stretch out above me
adjusting their shapes
to the shape I made
in the sheets
beneath them on the dusty floor
I fall asleep
in the empty sack of my skin

Renting My Bed to the Bones

I have rented my bed
to the bones
they came saying they needed
a place to sleep
all night I dug in the dark
working my way around stones
pulling up roots of trees
clearing the plot
at last the earth opened
like water
when the hole was wide enough
and deep breathing
evenly in the dark air
the bones stepped
into it like owners
and lay down
they shifted their weight
slightly to find
a comfortable rest and then
fell asleep I covered
them over with the soft earth
and left the rent
will not be due for years

When we sleep
they think we have died

When we awaken
they believe in miracles

When we hide
they look for us

When we die
they are born to the air

They say
where did he go

Not Many Years

Not many years from now
when they dig through the debris
they will find a stone
among the bones
and not knowing what
they are looking for
or finding have found
they will throw it away
never realizing
how deep the bones dug
to find the stone
never stopping to listen
to what it is whispering
or see when they smash it
how the light
splinters

Oil

They add like oil
and loose their own designs

they fall into heaps

the heaps begin to grow like weeds gone to seed

they dare the wind
to stop speaking of them

And If Shriven at Last We Rise

And if shriven at last we rise
and our parts report as promised
to fly through the air
and sing like some winged instrument
then let it be like the breath
we took and gave in life
like the rivers of air we drank
or the death we died to
without pain or pause
unnoticed until it was over

The Bones at Rest

Now the bones are at rest
no one need know where they go
or what they dream to do

the bones are at rest content

perhaps they are dead
perhaps they are only asleep

no doubt they will never return
to haunt our dreams as they have

for now anyhow it is over
this endless emptying
this filling

so much like what we name breath

IV

In a Room

It is like smoke escaping through a screened
window. When you enter an empty room,
with a chair in the center, when you
sit on the chair, waiting, and nothing happens,
and no one comes, you begin to notice
the size and shape of the room, the color,
or lack of color, of the walls, the cracks
in the floor beneath your feet, the ceiling
above you. After a time, when nothing
has happened and you have run out of ideas,
you look for the door. When you discover
that it has disappeared you begin to search
for it. You are certain there was a door,
reasonably certain you entered the room
through a door. When you cannot find it,
you sit down on the chair in the center
of the room. You wait for someone to come,
or to call. You notice, now, how the room
has begun to grow smaller, darker.

That House, This Room

Except for this thin flame the room
would not exist or need to be named.
No one could know, to prove it,
that we were even there. The wind,
in its own windows, rattles what frames
there are. The fire turns a chimney
of wind back to a tree remembering wind,
remembering leaves. The leaves turn
in the wind; the wind catches fire.
You, close, in the chair in the corner,
stir, turn. We both begin to speak
at once. The wind, like a tree on a hill,
begins to burn. There is nothing to know
that house, this room.

A Room without Windows

There is no decay. Nothing stays
like this. Therefore, no one wonders to look.
The way trees grow in one's room as he drinks
from a cup of coffee . . . When such things
happen, such trees, for instance, begin
to grow in your room, you do not notice,
and fail, even, to mind these facts
when they are pointed out to you on your
own blackboard, filled with shadows
of leaves, stirred by the breath of the speaker
speaking to you, pointing with his bony hand,
its finger his chalk, at the blackboard.

You sit quietly, bored, restless, wondering
your own thoughts, such as they are, or
can be, in a room so arranged. It is
as if you do not remember buying the furniture
or the people you invite to use it.
You stare at the ink-spill on the sofa,
shaped like an ear. The broken glass in the corner,
even though you cut your foot upon it,
seems only a moment of confused sunlight
in a room without windows.

A Short History of Misunderstanding

If you wish to be certain of misunderstanding
anything, experience it, hands sweaty
like any pubescent boy in the backseat of his father's car
his first time with a girl almost old enough
to know enough to. But this is the way the world goes,
one hat after another, until you go
bald and have to go out and find a hairpiece
that matches the fringe you have left,
around the edges, over the ears,
mostly gray, the one hair color in short supply.

So you try dye and end up painting the tops
of your ears an indelible bluey black,
the color of worn-out horses and
indiscriminate pelts worn by old women in hot weather.

Still, before the window closes on the wrong corner
of the moon, remember to keep your distance,
your palette poised and all the colors ready.
Try to avoid mixing. Stick with the primaries but
be alert at all times since you never know
when the mirror will stand up before you and a hand reach
around and under your eyelid and begin to pull
your scalp off or, just as interesting,
the girl so uncomfortable on the seat beside you,
her hands as sweaty as yours, begin to cry.

Cultivation of Pain

Put your hand into flame and hold it,
the pain like blood burning, five seconds,
ten if you can. You must learn this.
Call it cultivation of pain.

Practice standing in front of speeding cars.
Test your weight against bridges.
Buy a gun. Depending on your own individual
habits, it will take your whole life
to cultivate enough pain.

Snow

We are left, finally, to decide why
the world goes, and we with it,
toward some strange kind of return.

This morning, before morning, I dreamed
of snow falling thickly through trees.
When I awakened, snow was falling.

I put on the shoes of separation,
took the road of wandering, and walked out
to find a red heifer unblemished.

I spoke my name to the mountain
and waited to hear a word returned.
Nothing but the wind moved.

In less than an hour my tracks
were covered over, and still the snow
fell thick through the cedars

like dust, dust that at last would rise.

The Time of Year, the Hour

Snow is falling in the mountains.
For many miles wolves run without resting,
their breath like long scarves of blood.

It is the time of year, the hour,
when things cross and cross again; knock
without knowing they stand before the door.

The fire has found its lost wing,
and the end of the journey, like a shadow
of old shoes, stands waiting to be stepped into.

Water forgets its wounds.
The light has opened its long hands.
Even the dead have stopped dying.

Short Treatise on the Hand

The first empirical reality, untouchable
in its metaphysic, integer
to the whole body, better than the eye
for ultimate knowledge of the personality,
first witness to death,
the most washed and least clean
of all members of the human body,
the hand busies itself with revenge.

As the handshake originated in mistrust,
so it is often misused, signifying,
simultaneously, greeting,
farewell, promise, praise, pardon . . .

Beware of the man who comes toward you
with his hand extended.
Examine him as carefully
as you would examine a fly on the lid
of your coffin.

The Place of Lost Breath

I have dug a deep hole for the drum
of my heartbeat and put it into the hole
and thrown dirt in upon it and stones.

Later when I came back to pay my respects
I found the place only with difficulty
because there was no marker and savage tribes

had set up a circle of fires around the spot
and I had to open a vein in my arm and
show blood to enter again that holy place.

Breakfast as a Last Resort

When, some morning, early, at breakfast
upon the patio overlooking the river gorge,
the walls of rock alive in the white sun,
you drop your hand to drink from your coffee
and, reaching, spy beneath the glass-topped table
your feet like boats of death . . .

                              In times like these,
when the world has stopped believing in the possibility
of a future, when there is such energy for evil
which way you turn, there is nothing to do but turn
back to the conversation about the sunrise, the
vistas forward and back, here and there, what
travels you have. Yes, drink from the cup of coffee
and smile at the waitress in the short dress,
who smiles, who doesn't understand your language.

When it is all over and past time to depart,
let the hour ring clearly in the antique clock,
while you hesitate, your hand with the cup of coffee
just to your lips, the end of a sentence brushing
around it. The driver is always impatient, but waits,
whistling, his foot on the running board, cap
tilted over one eye, smiling; he will wait. Place
your empty cup carefully on the ring of its reflection
in the dark glass, straighten your tie, wink
at the waitress on the way out, to the waiting car.